On Display

ON DISPLAY

25 Themes to Promote Reading

by Gayle Skaggs

McFarland & Company, Inc., Publishers
Jefferson, North Carolina, and London

This book is dedicated to my daughters,
Betsy and Sarah,
and to the faculty, staff and students
of Ezard Elementary School

Cover design by Robert L. Skaggs.

British Library Cataloguing-in-Publication data are available

Library of Congress Cataloguing-in-Publication Data

Skaggs, Gayle, 1952–
    On display : 25 themes to promote reading / by Gayle Skaggs.
        p.   cm.
    Includes index.
    ISBN 0-7864-0657-7 (sewn softcover : 55# alkaline paper) ∞
    1. School libraries—United States. 2. Library exhibits—United
States.   3. Displays in education.   I. Title.
Z675.S3S5975   1999
027.8'074'73—dc21   98-54964 CIP

Manufactured in the United States of America

McFarland & Company, Inc., Publishers
  Box 611, Jefferson, North Carolina 28640

CONTENTS

Contents

FOREWORD

Here at Ezard Elementary it is no surprise that one of the favorite student hangouts is the library. For here students are often greeted by a smiling life-size "Garfield" or beckoned by "Snoopy" to enter into a magical world of an enchanted castle with its very own life-like dragon or a wondrous underwater adventure full of colorful fish and strange creatures reading some very interesting books. These are just a few of the numerous themes Mrs. Skaggs has developed to help create an inviting and exciting environment for our library.

Mrs. Skaggs has a gift for developing ideas that entice students to enter the library. Once the students are "lured" in, they are often pleasantly surprised to find that there are books for everyone, regardless of their interests. Although the students are having fun they are also learning, quite often without even knowing it. The original and interesting themes have made reading come alive for the students of Ezard Elementary.

Tom Hibbs, Principal
Ezard Elementary School
Conway, Missouri

1

PREFACE

Learning to read is one of the most exciting events in a person's life. Encouraging and maintaining that excitement is often quite a challenge for any librarian or classroom teacher.

This book offers ideas for displays designed to promote reading. The displays are arranged by themes. The majority of these themes can be used at any time of the year, though a few are more seasonal. At first glance, you may think that these are only for elementary age students, but please give them a second look. Many of the ideas can be used with any age group simply by varying the books that are displayed. Try the ideas as presented, or use your own creativity to adapt these to better meet your needs. Consider combining several of the ideas to create an even better one. The possibilities are endless and exciting.

INTRODUCTION: GETTING STARTED

When you hear the words "bulletin board," a particular image probably comes to your mind. This might be a pleasant thought of a past successful display, or it might be a horror story that has come back to haunt you. Bulletin boards can be fun to create and can become that special spark needed to liven up a dull space. Put all your old ideas about displays away and concentrate on using new and different materials, bold colors and more 3-D displays.

Begin by looking at your display space. Can you possibly stretch the area to include an entire wall? Is it possible to hang things from the ceiling? Assess the display limitations and then focus on the possibilities. Try to use the space in a different way or use space that you have not previously used for displays. Look for some small areas such as the top or end of a bookshelf, a window sill, a support post, etc., for a place to get started.

To create a bulletin board in a new space or an odd-sized area, use a piece of ¾" or ½" foam insulation. This is available at a lumber yard in 4' × 8' sheets at a very low cost. Use a matte knife or utility knife to cut it to size and simply hang it with a couple of pieces of heavyweight fishing line. This bulletin board can be moved quickly and easily as the need arises.

Do not try to display a lot of things at one time. Keep the area uncluttered with a few well designed displays that are changed frequently. Changing things every three to four weeks will keep your patrons guessing and looking forward to what you will come up with next. This will keep the room more exciting for you as well.

5

As you plan your bulletin board, keep in mind that people will pass by it quickly, which requires the message to be relatively simple and direct. They may not notice all the subtle little details for a few days. You may want to repeat your theme phrase over and over throughout the library.

If your school has a mascot, try to use it whenever possible. This will personalize each display and your patrons will see that it was designed especially for them and wasn't a mass-produced item.

It isn't necessary to spend a lot of money for materials. Use whatever is available in a creative way. Many of the ideas in this book are made with carpet tubes. These are available free of charge at most carpet stores. Although they come 12' long, they can be cut with a saw to any length.

All materials should be clean, bright, neat and always safe. Recycle and reuse the pieces over and over in new combinations. Black plastic bags work well for storage because they keep the sunlight from the construction paper and protect it from fading.

This is your space so relax and enjoy yourself!

Backgrounds

Lots of materials work well for display backgrounds. These are just a few suggestions:

- Poster paper or large sheets of construction paper
- Wrapping paper or gift wrap
- Paper or plastic tablecloths
- Brown mailing paper
- Newspaper, especially the comics or the classifieds
- Fabric such as burlap or denim
- Old bed sheets
- Plastic bags—usually black or blue
- Wallpaper
- Newsprint
- Cardboard

Visuals

Use an opaque projector if you have trouble drawing some of the items suggested. Some could be enlarged on the copy machine to serve as patterns. Try to use the idea of folding the paper and drawing half the object on the fold. This will help you create a symmetrical pattern.

Fishing line is the best material for hanging items. It is inexpensive and is almost invisible. Open up a paper clip to use as a hook to attach the artwork to a light fixture or ceiling tile.

As previously stated, try to personalize your displays whenever possible. If your school has a mascot or specific school colors, try to work these in if the opportunity arises. This will pique interest and help to grab the attention of your students or patrons.

Lettering

Use clear, easy-to-read letters. Sloppy lettering can ruin an otherwise wonderful display. Always check your spelling and use correct punctuation.

Computer-generated letters are acceptable, but consider the old-fashioned way of cutting out the letters from a wide variety of paper types. Letter patterns can be purchased, or you can create your own. Look at the fonts on your computer. Choose the one you like best and print off the alphabet in the appropriate size. Use these for patterns. Vary the size, color and style of the letters. Use lower case as well as upper case letters or the combination to keep the displays interesting.

Keep your eyes open for new ways to use whatever materials are readily available to you. It won't be long before you will be soaking up lots of compliments on your displays.

1

READ &
ROCK & ROLL

The 1950s have always been popular, and the era offers many great decorating possibilities. Most people associate the decade with Rock & Roll, poodle skirts, hula hoops and Elvis. Take advantage of these icons to generate some real excitement in your library or classroom.

A simple bulletin board would be a great start if you have only a small space to dedicate to this project. This theme is pretty addictive, however, and will probably just naturally expand.

Limit the number of colors in your display. Try using a primary color scheme of red, blue and yellow with black for details. Using a yellow background, feature red letters for a bold message about reading. Blue books with white pages work well. Black is the natural color for the records and the music notes.

A border for this particular display is not necessary. Using fishing line, hang additional music notes around the edges of the bulletin board to give the whole display more depth and pizzazz.

The records (45s) are 7" in diameter and are made from black poster board or heavy black paper with labels of yellow or light blue. Write the names of books or 50s songs on the labels, or just leave them blank. Laminating will give them the shine of a real record and also prolong their life. Do the same for the music notes.

Almost all 50s decorating includes a jukebox. This can be as com-plicated or as simple as you desire. The easiest way to make one is to create a front view only of the jukebox. Use a large sheet of cardboard or a sheet of heavy paper. Make as large a rectangle from this mater-ial as possible. Round off one end to serve as the top of the jukebox. (See the drawing on the next page.)

JUKEBOX #1

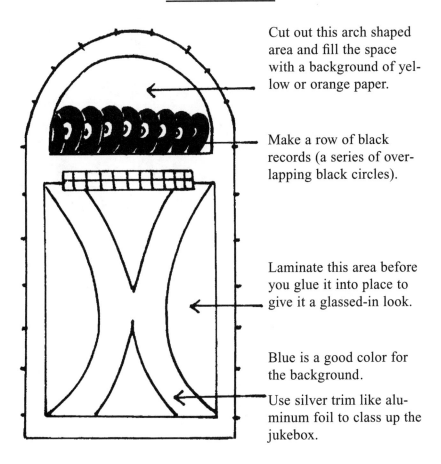

Cut out this arch shaped area and fill the space with a background of yellow or orange paper.

Make a row of black records (a series of overlapping black circles).

Laminate this area before you glue it into place to give it a glassed-in look.

Blue is a good color for the background.

Use silver trim like aluminum foil to class up the jukebox.

Outline the display with a string of white or colored lights. Slip in a cassette player or CD player in an inconspicuous location and play some 50s music. Play music during designated times each day such as before school or during the lunch hour. This will really pep up your day, and you will miss the music greatly when you move on to your next display.

JUKEBOX #2

Use a refrigerator box for this large size jukebox. Cut the box in half vertically using a matte knife or utility knife.

Stretch a piece of heavy colored paper across the top of the arch. Attach with staples to each side.

Cut an arched top on the front of the box. Cut out this arch shaped area and fill the space by following the directions given for Jukebox #1.

This will fit up against the wall.

Leave the bottom in the box to help the jukebox maintain its shape.

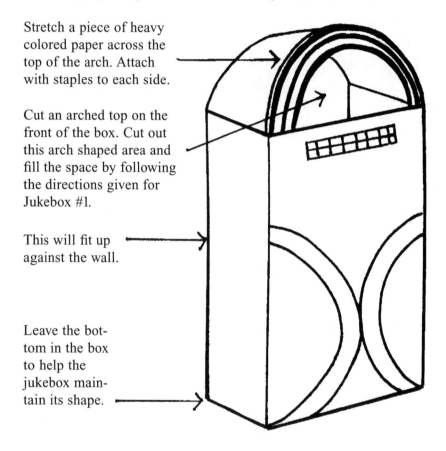

Paint the box a color such as blue. The area around the arch looks great done in a rainbow stripe. Use some aluminum foil to add some flashy trim. White or colored lights look great outlining your jukebox.

For a long wall, use the theme title cut from red or black letters. Use a large font in addition to music notes, records, possibly some hearts and some dancing books.

Music notes can also be made from paper towel tubes. This will create a free standing music note.

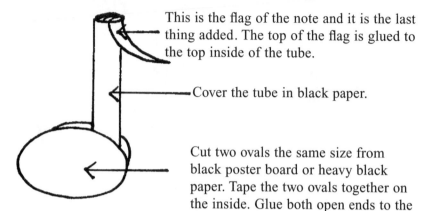

This is the flag of the note and it is the last thing added. The top of the flag is glued to the top inside of the tube.

Cover the tube in black paper.

Cut two ovals the same size from black poster board or heavy black paper. Tape the two ovals together on the inside. Glue both open ends to the tube. Be sure to stand up the tube on a table or other flat surface when gluing on the ovals. The ovals serve as a sort of training wheel for the tube to keep it upright.

These standing notes can also serve as centerpieces for tables or to decorate the top of a bookcase. Flowers or balloons on sticks can be inserted in the top of the note to add more color and pizzazz.

Consider hanging these notes with fishing line around the room. Gigantic notes could be made in the same way using carpet tubes in place of the paper towel tube.

Some other activities for this theme might include:

1. Sponsor an all-school dress-up day focusing on the 50s.
2. Display photographs of people from the 1950s. This could be worked into a trivia contest or reference project. "Faces of the 50s"
3. Display pictures of people hula-hooping, cramming into telephone booths and doing other 50s fad activities.
4. Feature biographies of people such as Harry S Truman, Marilyn Monroe, Dwight Eisenhower, and Elvis Presley.
5. Display a time line of the 50s.
6. Display cartoon or comic strips from the 50s.
7. Feature web sites like the Rock & Roll Hall of Fame.

8. Feature Caldecott or Newbery books from the 50s.
9. Display your school's yearbooks from the 50s.

There are so many great phrases to use in your displays. Look in your high school's old yearbooks and see what phrases were used in your area. Try this one:

PICKIN' THE HITS

This theme works well any time of the year and is lots of fun. Many of your younger students may not know what a record is. Here is your opportunity to share some of the great things of the past with today's students.

2

THE JUNGLE

This jungle theme can be simple or complicated depending upon your needs. A jungle is full of activity and life just as a library, or classroom, is an active, busy place. Use lots of green leaves, bright flowers, animals, palm trees, etc. If space is available, bring in live plants to decorate and add authenticity to your jungle motif.

The main emphasis of this theme is to stress the importance of developing good library skills. Wading through information can at times seem like fighting your way through a jungle. Feature the most important parts of the library such as the reference section, the card catalog, and all the on-line resources available.

The bulletin board on the following page sums up the theme for the month, "It can be a jungle out there without good library skills!" Position this in your most attention-getting location and try to work in a larger format than you usually do. It's fine to extend beyond the borders of a bulletin board. Consider using an entire wall. Think big!

The background works well when done in black or a very dark blue paper. The dark background will make it seem a little scary and ominous besides making the colorful leaves and flowers stand out.

Use red or yellow letters along with lots of green leaves of varying types and some colorful tissue paper flowers. The snakes can be made from construction paper or use rubber snakes and a rubber spider for a more 3-D look.

IT CAN BE A JUNGLE OUT THERE WITHOUT GOOD LIBRARY SKILLS!

If you have the space, add a few palm trees. These can easily be made with carpet tubes. Carpet tubes are usually free at carpet or flooring stores and can be cut to any desired length with a saw. Use scrap lumber to make a base for each palm tree. Nail three boards together as shown in the illustration.

Nail two boards together to create an X shape. Nail a third smaller board at the center of the X so that it can stand up inside the carpet tube. Use two small scraps of wood to balance the X shape.

Set the tube down onto the short vertical board. Nail or put screws through the tube into the board to secure it in place.

Cover the entire base area in brown mailing paper to make it more attractive. Cut strips of brown mailing paper and fringe one side. Wrap these up the entire length of the trunk.

Straighten out wire coat hangers. Use pliers to close the sharp end into a circle so as to protect anyone from walking into this sharp end. Bend the other end to resemble the illustration below. This will allow you to slide the wire onto the top of the tube to attach the leaves.

Using a large sheet of green paper, cut an elongated football shape the length of one of your pieces of wire. Cut this shape in a zigzagged pattern to resemble a leaf. Carefully tape the paper on to one of the wires prepared according to the previous directions. Use magic tape and use it sparingly because you do not want the tape to be obvious. These leaves can then be bent and shaped to form an interesting tree. Use approximately five leaves for each tree.

Wad up some small brown paper lunch bags to form coconuts. Use a black marker to add the appropriate coconut markings. Position two or three in your tree top. These can be taped in place or can be secured with fishing line.

You can make monkeys and birds if you want or just use stuffed animals. They will be just as effective and can be secured in place with fishing line.

To create a great snake, use an old piece of hose from a vacuum cleaner. Add a styrofoam ball for the head.

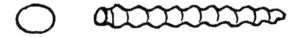

Use white duct tape to cover the entire ball and attach it to the hose. Spray paint the snake and glue on some paper eyes or use a permanent marker to draw on eyes. Add a cut paper tongue.

A snake could also be made with one leg of a pair of panty hose. Stuff this with fiberfill or some form of stuffing. Form a head and then spray paint your creation.

Coil your snake around in the tree and secure it in place by tying it with fishing line.

For a ceiling area, unwrap an old grapevine wreath and stretch it out securing it in place by tying the branches to some part of the ceiling with fishing line.

Cut leaves from green tissue paper and tape them to the grapevine. Add some large bright tissue paper flowers. These can be made by using three sheets of tissue paper any size and all one color or three different colors. Begin at one end folding the paper back and forth accordion style.

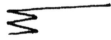

Continue this all the way across the paper.

Use a twist-tie and wrap it tightly around the middle of the folded paper.

Begin on one side by slowly pulling up the first sheet toward the twist-tie.

Pull up the top sheet on the other side. Pull these to the center folding one side around the other.

Repeat the process until all the layers have been pulled up. Carefully move the tissue paper around to form a flower. These can be attached to green ribbon and hung around the room or draped through the hanging grapevine.

Use animal posters or photographs of African animals. Think up library or book related things for these animals to say. Write these on cartoon-like balloons and carefully attach them to the photographs. Some examples of these might be:

- So….where are the books about Michael Jordan? (Said by jumping tree frogs)
- Honest, I remember I returned that book! (Said by an elephant)
- What was that web site again?
- Check this out!
- Could someone point out the hair care books? (An ape might say this)
- Where are the joke books? (Hyena material for sure!)

Add some butterflies around your flowers. Fold a piece of construction paper in half. Draw half a butterfly on the fold.

Cut while the paper is folded. Open out the wings.

Use black paper to make the body and head shape. Glue this along the fold of the wings.

Cut two long strips of black paper to serve as antennae. Use contrasting colors of paper to decorate the wings or use markers to draw in areas of color.

These butterflies can be hung from the ceiling on fishing line or taped to the wall.

Around the room feature large green leaves with library skills or types of reference listed on them. Letters can be cut from paper or the word simply written in with black marker.

Feature books on the rain forest, jungle birds and animals, the Amazon area, acid rain and ecology. This fits in well with Earth Day activities.

3

KEEP ON TRACK...

Use a blue background to boldly display your train. Cut out a simple black engine silhouette from construction paper and the letters to spell the word "READ." Use small black circles for the train wheels. Cut out a large white cloud shape on which to display the theme title.

Trains are still interesting and exciting to children. Feature books on trains and model trains.

Display books in a train-like fashion. Make an engine from black poster board and tape it to a bookend. A back brace can be made for the engine if a bookend is not available. Make a triangular shape from posterboard or cardboard similar to the one in the illustration below. Fold along the dotted line and glue to the back of the engine shape. This can be the lead for a grouping of books.

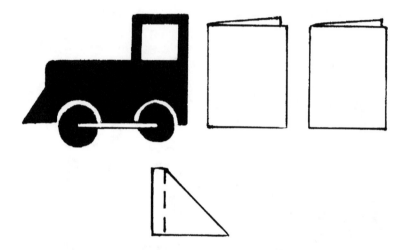

These are some train books to feature for your younger readers:

Shortcut.
Catch Me, Catch Me!
The Caboose Who Got Loose.
The Little Engine That Could.
The Sunday Outing.

Put masking tape on the floor to resemble train tracks. Start at the door and set down tracks leading directly to the checkout desk or to your book display. Contact Amtrac or your local train carrier and request train safety handouts, posters and banners, possibly even some paper engineer hats.

Create a banner to display in your computer area such as the one on the next page. On a blue background, use bright colors with the name of each search engine done in a different color. Use black for the engine and the words "SEARCH ENGINES." Add additional search engines to fill an entire wall.

Make reader crossing signs from white poster board strips to use in doorways. These signs can be actually taped on the door or hung on a free-standing carpet tube. (See the directions for making a palm tree in Chapter 2 to get instructions for tube base). Paint the tube black or cover it in black paper. Add a couple of red circles to simulate lights.

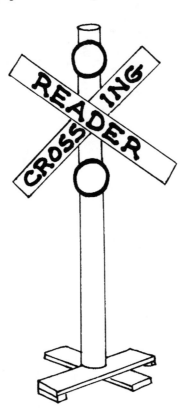

Search Engines

webcrawler – yahoo – AltaVista

4

PIG OUT ON READING

Pigs seem to bring a smile to most people. "Ham it up" with large pink cardboard or pink paper pigs. Use an opaque projector to reproduce an illustration of a pig from a favorite book or draw one on your own. Don't be concerned about making your pig look realistic but try for a cartoon-look.

The key is to make these pigs big. Give them books, newspapers or magazines to read. Promoting reading is the whole key!

Use your favorite pig in a relaxed pose to feature on a bulletin board such as the one on the next page. The background color looks best if dark such as black, blue or purple. Pink looks great for the pig and the letters. Pink is a great theme color to use anytime you feature a pig or the word pig. You could use a book jacket or paperback or even a magazine in place of the paper books as shown in the drawing.

To add to the pig theme, make pig heads to hang around the room. Use two pink paper plates and construction paper for each pig head. Use the back side of the paper plates. Using pink construction paper, cut a slightly flattened pink circle for the nose. Use a black marker to add two nostrils. Cut two small black construction paper circles and glue them on for eyes.

Cut two ears from pink construction paper. Fold a piece of 9" × 12" paper in half. Draw a rounded triangle shape for the ear. Cut this shape out while the paper is folded to end up with two ears the same size. Put a small pleat in the ear shape to give it a more 3D shape.

Staple the two plates together. Slide the ear in the space between the two plates and staple in place. Bend the top of the ear down.

Rafia can be added to resemble straw. Hang using fishing line.

If you do not wish to use paper plates, use two circles of pink construction paper that are the same size. Staple the two together going about three-fourths of the way around and then stuff the opening with small pieces of wadded-up newspaper. This will give the shape a little padding. Insert the ears as described previously and finish stapling.

To decorate the doorway, make a sign that says something like "Hog Heaven" or "Porkin' Out" or even "We Pig Out on Books Here," etc. A banner might be made that says "Go ahead, make a pig of yourself. Read ALL our books! You just can't get enough of good books!"

A great door swag can be made from pink paper plates. Make two pig heads as previously described. You will use one on each end. Cut out the letters of the word READ from pink paper plates, one letter per plate.

Punch a hole in the side of each pig head. Tie a piece of fishing line between the two pig heads. Tape the letters on to the fishing line so that the tape does not show and the letters will hang nicely. Tie rafia between the letters and around the pigs to look like straw. This will look very cheerful and will be a great way to greet your patrons.

Create book displays on table tops or possibly on the wall if display pegboard is available to you. This could be referred to as the "Pig Pen." A fence made of construction paper, posterboard or purchased fence borders adds to the theme. Feature books about pigs that are fiction or nonfiction—farm books, drawing books, even pig poems. This is a neat time to show that pig information is available all over the library. These are some great pig books to showcase:

Pigs Aplenty, Pigs Galore.
Pigs in Space.
The Pig's Wedding.
Pigsty.
Pigs in the Mud in the Middle of the Rud.

5

UNDERWATER THEME

Are you looking for an opportunity to display your Titanic books? Go for a total underwater theme.

To give the space a water look, use large blue plastic trash bags. Cut the bags open to create big sheets of blue plastic. Fasten these with tape or thumb tacks along the top of the walls of your display space. They will move a little as people pass by and this makes the display seem more alive. This can also be used to create a background for a bulletin board.

For the bulletin board idea on the next page, use blue paper or blue plastic for the background. Use brown construction paper to create the treasure chest. The base of the chest is simply a rectangle with lines drawn in with a black marker. Another slightly smaller rectangle will work for the lid but you will need to round off the two smaller sides. Add a little aluminum foil for fancy trim. The books can be made from construction paper or use some paperback books or magazines instead.

Use some yellow or orange construction paper for the fish. Details can be added in marker or contrasting colors of paper. Green crepe paper or paper ribbon creates the illusion of seaweed. Actual shells or even a starfish add some authenticity to the display.

Opening a book is like
opening a treasure chest.

Make large fish to hang from the ceiling. A fish is made from two sheets of construction paper stapled together with a small amount of newspaper inside for padding. A fish is just a football shape with a tail and fins. Add construction paper eyes and use a black marker to draw on the scales. Glue the two larger fins on so that they can flop around. If you don't like the look of the staples, stitch the two sheets of paper together using a sewing machine. This looks good and is easy to do.

Use fishing line to hang the fish around the room. Intersperse green crepe paper or ribbon among the fish to serve as seaweed. For added atmosphere, play tapes of the sounds of ocean waves, etc. This may make your room so restful that you find yourself nodding off.

This is a great time to introduce an aquarium into your library or classroom. It would be a good way to explain fiction and nonfiction using the real fish and your handmade fish as obvious examples. Feature books on sharks, fish, sunken ships and lost treasures, scuba diving, submarines and even trout fishing.

To feature your electronic media, use a large fish net suspended from the ceiling. Print off the addresses for some interesting net sites. Laminate them and suspend them from the net. Your students will enjoy visiting these sites.

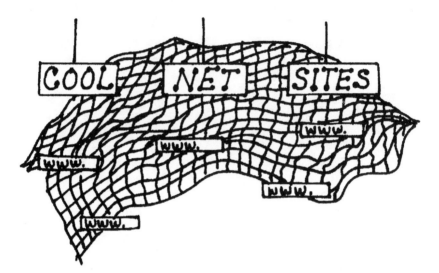

6

YOUR STATE

Students need to know more about their home state and this can become the basis for a great celebration whether in just your area or school-wide. Research your state to determine if there is an official state day. The third Wednesday of October is Missouri Day.

Using Missouri as an example, these are some suggestions to feature your state and to celebrate its heritage.

1. Use a map of your state on a bulletin board and mark the home towns of authors that are well known to your students. See the bulletin board on the following page as an example. Use a color scheme that matches the colors of the state flag. Maintain this color scheme in all your decorating. Feature books by these authors in a colorful display.

2. Research the names of famous people from your state and photocopy some of their pictures for display. Laminating the photos will increase their life. Feature biographies of these individuals.

3. Choose a famous individual from your state to pretend to be for the day and dress as they would. This might be Jesse James or Laura Ingalls Wilder if you are from Missouri. Your students will like dressing up. Distribute name tags for everyone to use and have them choose a person to pretend to be so that no one will feel left out of the celebration if they cannot dress up.

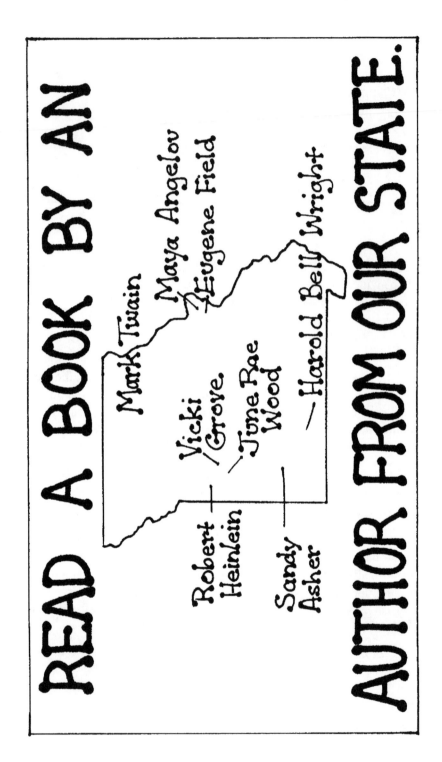

READ A BOOK BY AN AUTHOR FROM OUR STATE.

Mark Twain

Maya Angelou

Eugene Field

Harold Bell Wright

Vicki Grove

June Rae Wood

Robert Heinlein

Sandy Asher

4. For a school-wide celebration, assign to each classroom a town or city within your state for them to study in depth and pretend to be. Put a city limits sign outside each classroom featuring the city's name. Contact the chamber of commerce or tourist bureau of these towns for information and brochures. Many towns will even send free advertising merchandise for your students to promote tourism for their area.

5. Host a movie marathon of videos about your state whether historical or just travel information.

6. Invite your governor, senator, representative or mayor to come for a while to join in the celebration, possibly reading his/her favorite book to a class. This will give them an opportunity to talk to the children about their job and allow the students to ask questions. Our students were most impressed that their congressman cared enough about them that he would travel such a distance to visit our school.

7. Make a welcome banner for the building entrance. This design could work well for any state.

8. For the school's entrance, make a cool road sign pointing the way to your state's big cities. Use a carpet tube sitting on a base of three boards. Follow the directions for constructing a palm tree as shown in Chapter 2 which are the same directions needed to make this road sign. Cover the tube in whatever color paper fits your color scheme. Add a colorful red heart on top. This goes well with the welcome banner plan just given.

9. Coordinate the event with your school's art teacher. Art projects could be done to feature your state's flag, state bird, flower, tree, seal, etc. Display these in the hall for all to see.

10. Make pins for your faculty and staff to wear for the celebration. Find a cookie cutter shaped like your state. My school cafeteria had one shaped like Missouri, so check your cafeteria first. Follow this easy recipe for bread dough pins (Everyone will be so impressed with these!):

BREAD DOUGH PINS

The materials you need are white bread, white glue, dish soap, craft paint, polyurethane and pin backs.

Work with six slices of bread, first cutting off the crusts. (Feed the crusts to your dog or to the birds.) Crumble the bread into a bowl, adding six teaspoons of white glue. (Use the same number spoons of glue as you use slices of bread.) Add a squirt of dishsoap. This adds glycerin to the mixture and dishsoap is an inexpensive source for glycerin.

Use your hands to mix this goop together. Knead the mixture until it becomes smooth and somewhat elastic.

Use a rolling pin to roll out the dough to about 1/8" thick. Cut out shapes with your cookie cutter or use sharp scissors to cut out the desired shapes. Smooth out the edges with your fingers. Allow these to dry for at least three days, remembering to flip them over periodically. The drying process causes them to warp if they are not turned over every once and awhile.

Paint these shapes with any craft paint and seal in polyurethane. Add a pin back by brushing over the base of the back with more polyurethane.

The Missouri pins were painted blue with a red heart painted on where our town is located. This could be done for your state, too.

11. What does your state's license plate look like? Make a copy of the design but replace the license numbers with Dewey Decimal numbers such as "300s" or "398.2." Make them a usable size, laminate if desired and display them on your shelves. A copy of the license plate for each state can be found in the cover pages of the *World Almanac for Kids*.

12. Create a wall-size tree display featuring one leaf for each county in your state. Missouri has 114 counties which were done in leaves of red, orange, yellow, brown and green construction paper. The county's name should be written on the leaf in black marker. The students were surprised to see how many 114 really was as opposed to just hearing the number. It made them all seem more real to the students. This was a very effective and colorful fall display.

7

A MYSTERY

Most of us love a good mystery. This can be a theme you will want to repeat year after year.

Starting in the hall, put down black construction paper footprints that lead right on in to your card catalog. The life of these will be longer if they are laminated. Use footprints with the Dewey numbers added in white to label your various nonfiction areas.

Just as at a crime scene, mark off the outline of a book (rather than the outline of a body). Use masking tape and go for any size. Add a big question mark to go along with the mystery theme.

The yellow caution tape used for construction or similar to the type used by the police at a real crime scene could be draped throughout the room. This could be used to draw attention to a specific part of the collection.

Host a trivia contest or create some interest in a famous unsolved mystery. Display mystery books whether fiction or nonfiction. Book talk some of these to build interest.

Make a simple banner like the one below in colors such as black and yellow or black and orange.

To create a bulletin board for this mystery theme, use photographs of well known authors. Cover up the names and create wanted posters. Photocopy these so that they really look like mug shots. Use an ISBN or LC number for one of their books as their prison number. Keep the whole display in black and white. Some popular authors to use are R.L. Stine, K.A. Applegate, Beverly Cleary and Gary Paulsen.

To be most effective, use black paper for the background with white letters. The illustration on the next page is done in reverse simply because it was easier to draw that way.

Use fishing line to hang large question marks around the room. A large question mark could be formed on the wall from the words who, what, when, where and why.

Consider creating a mystery in your own setting. This could be like a treasure hunt with clues placed in different areas of the library. Offer prizes such as bookmarks for all those who follow the clues leading them through the library's resources.

To get your students oriented to your library, host a mystery or introduction game with this activity. Give each student a pencil and a sheet of paper with the following categories listed:

Fiction _____

000–200 _____

300–400 _____

500 _____

600 _____

700 _____

800 _____

900 _____

92(Biography) _____

Have the students move through these areas of the library looking for a book whose title begins with one of their two initials. If their initials were G and S, they would look for books whose title begin with a G or an S.

This is a timed activity with a prize for the student finished in the shortest amount of time. It is important to check the titles before awarding a prize because many times the students get in such a hurry that they may pick up a book in the wrong Dewey number.

This activity is great for the beginning of the school year but be prepared for those tidy shelves to look a little messy.

8

GIVE YOURSELF
A GIFT

This theme is designed to promote reading and to think of books as gifts from the authors. It works well to complement your December decorating. The goal is to treat yourself to something special—a chance to read.

The bulletin board on the next page gets the message across but is still relatively simple. Use a plain background color with some bold red letters. The books can be made from construction paper with ribbon added or possibly some foil trim.

Get your patrons involved by giving each one a paper package on which they could write the title and author of their favorite book.

This is a wonderful time to have book talks. People love to talk about the books they've read, so offer the opportunity.

Display these all around the room or down a hallway. They can be used alone or glued on to a background sheet.

Choose some of these favorites to display. This can be done in many ways. One of the easiest ways would be to tie ribbon and bows around the actual books and just display them on top of a book shelf. A bow can be glued or taped onto a Popsicle stick and then slipped down easily inside a displayed book.

Use a large box or table and wrap it to look like a large gift. You might use regular gift wrap, poster paper or possibly some fabric such as a holiday tablecloth. Display books on the top. This type of arrangement makes it easier to check out the books because the ribbon, etc., is on the box, not the books.

Be sure to use a very sturdy box because you will not want the display to be wobbly.

To go with your Christmas decorating and to continue the gift idea, make large paper gifts and add the words Merry Christmas but do so in Spanish, French, Chinese, etc. Feature holiday information for these countries.

9

THINK SPRING!
FLOWER POWER!

Decorating for spring is such a treat after those wintertime blahs. Use lots of bright cheerful colors and think BIG. Start with gigantic flowers that are lifesize—about five feet tall. Try a display such as the one on the next page.

Make the head from a circle of foam insulation or foam packing covered in brown, yellow or orange paper. Use a sheet of posterboard to make the flower petals. Glue the foam center to the posterboard. Use a pair of old sunglasses and remove the ear pieces. Pin the glasses into place on the foam with straight pins. Glue on a big pair of red paper lips for the mouth.

Suspend the flower head from the ceiling with fishing line. Use green crepe paper or green construction paper for the flower's body. Cut two leaves to serve as hands and position them around a magazine, newspaper or lightweight book for the flower to be reading. These can be taped to the wall or pinned to the bulletin board.

If you have a good sense of humor, give your lifesize flower some of your own characteristics. I would be sure to give my flower red glasses because I wear them. They could even have a collar and neck-tie. The key to successful decorating is to have fun and don't be afraid to try something really different!

The large flower heads can just hang around the room without the stems. They add a little pizzazz to any corner.

Add more flowers by cutting simple daisy shapes from white posterboard and adding a yellow center to each side. Hang these with fishing line in an organized pattern. It will give your space a "70's" look with flower power.

These daisy shapes can also be stapled or taped together to create a daisy chain to hang around the room or use as a border for a bulletin board.

To add a 3-D flower to a bare area, make a daisy in a flower pot similar to the one on the next page. Start with a real clay flower pot. The size is not important. Put a piece of Styrofoam or florist foam in the bottom of the pot. Paint a drinking straw green to serve as the stem. Stand the straw up in the Styrofoam. Fill the pot with dirt or Spanish moss to hide the Styrofoam.

Use posterboard for the flower petals and add a colorful center. Leaves make great hands to possibly hold a small book for this flower to read.

To compliment your spring theme, add things like colorful kites, butterflies, ladybugs and even a large sun. The sun would look great wearing sunglasses to match the large flowers.

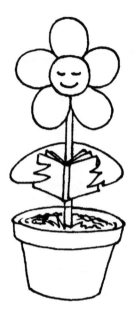

To create a 3-D butterfly, use a paper towel tube painted black for the body. Using a 12" × 18" piece of construction paper folded in half, draw half of the butterfly wings on the fold.

Cut while the paper is still folded. Open it out and decorate with colorful construction paper or simply decorate with markers.

Glue the tube to the center of the wings. Add two thin black strips slightly curled to create antennae. The wings can be bent and positioned in different ways.

This would be a great opportunity to feature gardening books, Earth Day information, kite making suggestions and books about spring holidays. These are some suggestions for younger readers.

Spring Is Here.
How Do You Know It's Spring?
What Happens in Spring?
Busy Bunnies.
Cranberry Easter.

10

POUNCE ON A
GOOD BOOK

People always have an opinion on cats; they seem to love them or despise them. Basing your display on cats will definitely get a response from your patrons.

For a bulletin board idea, try the one on the next page. Use a background such as blue with some bold red letters and darker blue books. Both cats could be the same color or opposites such as black and white. Keep all the parts very simple. The cats can be made easily using an opaque projector. Don't worry about realism.

Display fiction and nonfiction books about cats, kittens, lions and tigers, etc. These are a few to consider:

Cat in the Hat.
The Christmas Day Kitten.
Moses the Kitten.
Mother Halverson's New Cat.
Feathers for Lunch.
Millions of Cats.
Garfield Goes to Hollywood.
The Cricket in Times Square.
The Cat Who.......Lillian Braun's series.

Hang an appropriate banner to go with your displayed books. This sleeping cat would look great on a piece of blue paper with black or red lettering. Use one from an old calendar if you can't make one.

An easy way to decorate along the tops of bookshelves would be to use silhouettes of cats cut from black paper. Fold a 12" × 18" sheet of black paper in half. Draw half the cat on the fold. Cut this out while the paper is still folded. Add a tail. Use a variety of poses.

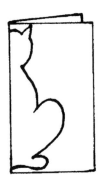

If drawing the outline of a cat is too much to try, consider using a cat cookie cutter and trace the shape on a sheet of paper. Enlarge this on the copy machine until you get the size you want. Use this as a pattern.

Cool cats can also be made using carpet tubes. Cut a tube approximately 12" long. Cover the tube in whatever color paper you want your cat to be.

Cut out a circle for the head with cut paper eyes, nose, ears and whiskers. The legs can be made with a piece of 12" × 18" paper folded in half. Cut them out while the paper is folded.

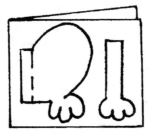

Fold along the line on the back leg and then glue it in place on the tube. Glue on the head and the front legs. Glue on a long tail that can be wrapped around.

When completed, set the cat with a book in front of it and position the paws around the book. A little bit of sticky tack will hold them in place and not damage the book.

It isn't even necessary to make an entire cat to create a great display item. Make a head and glue it on the carpet tube. Make two paws that can be taped around the book. Add a tail.

Another possibility would be to make a cat head from construction paper. Tape or glue it to a popsicle stick. Just slide the stick into a standing book and tape on some paws.

To add to this theme, make some cat heads to hang around the room. It would work to use paper plates but why not cut two circles the same size from your choice of construction paper? Staple about ¾ of the way around the circle and then stuff with small pieces of wadded-up newspaper. Staple the rest of the circle. Add some cut paper eyes, a nose, ears and whiskers. Draw on a mouth. Hang with fishing line.

To make a curled-up cat, start with a large oval for the cat's body. Add a circle for the head with cut paper ears, nose, eyes and whiskers. Add two paws which can be taped to the back side of the head. Cut a back leg piece and a tail from the same color paper.

Bend the cat to fit around the standing book. Use a little sticky tack or tape to hold the cat to the book.

Stuffed cats work well if you don't feel confident making some. Use balls of brightly colored yarn to pull the cats together for your display. Yarn can be spread throughout the room and will make your cats look very mischievous and playful.

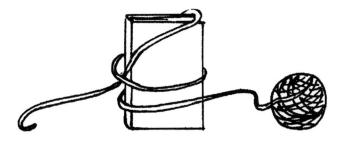

Some good phrases to use for this theme would be:

LIFE WITHOUT READING WOULD BE A "CAT"-ASTROPHE!

PURRRFECTLY WONDERFUL BOOKS.

PURRRSONAL FAVORITES.

Ask your patrons for the titles of their personal favorites and display these with a small little sign with their name on it.

11

BOOKS ADD COLOR
TO YOUR LIFE!

Everyone always likes everyday objects when they are made larger than normal size. Crayons are an important part of a child's life and work well to focus in on different parts of the library or classroom.

These large crayons are fun, quite easy to make and add a new dimension to a tired bulletin board. For the bulletin board on the next page, use a black background with the letters of the word "book" done in the same color as the large crayon. Use white letters for the remainder of the words so it will look like you have colored them in with the crayon. The crayon should be suspended from the ceiling with heavy weight fishing line.

The large crayon is made from a carpet tube covered in poster paper. Using a saw, cut the tube the length you would like your crayon to be. Cover one of the ends of the tube with a 12" square of paper in the color you would like your crayon to be. Carefully fold it down and tape it into place.

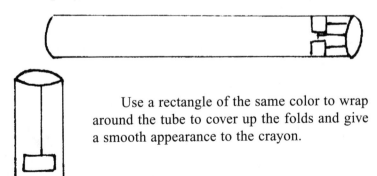

Use a rectangle of the same color to wrap around the tube to cover up the folds and give a smooth appearance to the crayon.

Use a sheet of 12" × 18" paper in the same color for the pointed end of the crayon. Roll this paper into a cone and staple it shut. Put small wads of newspaper into the cone to fill it up and help to maintain its shape.

Tape it in place as in the diagram.

Fold another sheet of the same color paper in half lengthwise. Wrap this around the part of the tube where the point meets the tube. This creates that special crayon-look.

Use a larger sheet of a contrasting color paper, such as pink or gray, to wrap around the tube for the crayon's label. Be sure this covers all the tape on both ends. Add all the little details to make this look like the real thing.

FICTION

Make a different crayon for each area of your library or for each subject taught in your classroom. An eight-pack of library colors could consist of fiction (yellow), easy fiction (brown), nonfiction (green), fairy tales or fantasy (purple), mystery (orange), scary (black), biography (blue), and reference (red). A classroom set might include reading, language arts, social studies, mathematics, science, art, music and physical education.

Hang these from the ceiling using fishing line to point out the usual locations for these books in the library. Use thin strips of the same color paper to create the illusion of a swipe of color.

Finish up the color display with stars from all eight colors that have been laminated. These look great hanging in a doorway. See the design on the next page.

Create an awning for the doorway using a tension rod to fit the door space. Drape a long strip of bright paper from the top of the door over the rod and then allow some to hang down. Tape stars to this awning and a swipe of color to match the color of the crayon on the wall by the door.

To create the wall-size crayon, use a large rectangle of paper in place of the carpet tube. Follow the directions previously given but simply make everything flat. This is a good opportunity to advertise the library. The colorful stars, along with the bright awning and swipe of color spanning the doorway, will be very attention getting and will brighten up the entire hallway.

Try a book display featuring books that have a color in the title such as:

Where the Red Fern Grows.
Green Eggs and Ham.
Anne of Green Gables.
Clifford the Big Red Dog.
A Taste of Blackberries.
The Witch of Blackbird Pond.
White Fang.

It's amazing how many titles have a color in them. Wrap yellow paper around a table to create a display space for your "color" books. This will resemble a crayon box. Add some simple letters.

12

OUTER SPACE

What's out there in outer space anyway? Feature information about the planets, stars, galaxies, NASA, space camp, astronauts, UFOs and anything else that you can think of. How about showcasing those Star Wars books or all the other great science fiction classics. Space, the final frontier, is a really big place so the subject matter is virtually endless.

Feature the NASA web site for all your Internet users. NASA will send you information to share with your patrons including posters and models to make.

To give a whole wall or the area above your bookshelves a look of the blackness of space, cut open black trash bags to create large sheets of black plastic or buy a roll of large black plastic. Tape the top of the plastic onto the wall where it meets the ceiling. This will work well as a backdrop for planets and stars. As part of the background, use lots of those little star stickers we love to use on charts.

Tape some planets and stars directly on the plastic and hang others on fishing line to create a more 3-D effect. It will be as though you are walking through outer space.

To create a simple but effective bulletin board, use black plastic for the background with the word READ done in yellow or gold stars. Hang additional stars around the bulletin board on fishing line.

Keep everything simple. It isn't necessary to make objects that are scientifically accurate. You are only going for the impression or the feel of space, not trying to make the technological equipment necessary to actually get there. Have fun with the theme!

Be sure that somewhere in the room you have a moon and a sun that are, of course, reading. This cool sun can be made with a piece of foam insulation cut into a circle and covered with yellow paper. Glue this circle on to a piece of yellow poster board cut into a sunray type of shape. Use a pair of old sunglasses with the ear pieces removed and pin them into place with straight pins. Add a smile with a marker. The book can be a magazine on outer space that is pinned into the foam for your sun to read.

Make the hanging objects very colorful. Laminating these will give them a great shine which will reflect the light and add a lot to the display.

Sponsor a filmfest of science fiction movies such as *The Empire Strikes Back, War of the Worlds, Star Trek* or an old episode of "Lost in Space." Host a trivia contest of old space movies or television programs. Who were some of your old "space" heroes?

Research some interesting facts about outer space to display or ask a class of students to do this research. This will let you know what they think is an interesting fact! These might include the distance from Pluto to Earth or the average temperature of the sun. Print these on poster board and laminate them. Hang these facts with fishing line wherever you need a little something extra.

Outline your checkout desk or the top of the bookshelves in white lights. Lights always add excitement to any display.

To create an exciting display using lights, such as the one on the next page, use a large sheet of cardboard painted black. Draw off several constellations on the back (being sure to do them in reverse so that they will be correct on the front side). Make a hole where each star would be located. Insert a white light in each hole. Tape it to hold it into place. Use white letters for your message.

These are some possible display headings:

3-2-1 BLAST OFF—READ!

MAY THE FORCE BE WITH YOU— READ!

ROCKET INTO READING!

THE SKY'S NOT
THE LIMIT!
READ

Any of those display headings would work with a simple bulletin board plan featuring rocket ships made from book jackets or photocopies of books that have been colored with markers. Add a few pieces of construction paper to create rockets or spaceships. Use a piece of black paper for the background or a piece of black plastic.

13

BOOKWORMS

For a small area that just needs a little pizzazz, add a bookworm. See the illustration on the next page for a bookworm bulletin board. This critter is made from a piece of dryer hose with a styrofoam ball for the head.

A 36" piece of dryer hose is a good length for the worm.

Use a 4" styrofoam ball to form the head with a 1" foam ball cut in half to make eyes. Straight pins will hold the styrofoam pieces together. Use white duct tape to cover the entire foam ball and to secure it to the dryer hose. Spray paint the worm any color you choose. Paint the eyeballs white with black added for the pupils.

Use pipe cleaners for antennae. A child's pair of sunglasses with the lens removed makes a wonderful pair of glasses for your worm. Draw a simple smile with a black permanent marker. To finish, add a bowtie.

Use your bookworm on a bulletin board or suspend it from the ceiling with fishing line.

The worm also looks great on your bulletin board in a large red apple. He certainly will give a great welcome to all who visit your room.

A possible caption for your book display might be:

**READERS INCH THEIR WAY TO SUCCESS
ONE BOOK AT A TIME**

Spread these words out in a worm-like fashion.

READ TO SUCCEED!

You will soon discover many different ways to display this bookworm. Use him stretched out to full length or squish him up to be partially hidden in a book or apple. Consider creating a whole group of these little guys.

Read To Succeed!

14

BASKETBALL

This is a great theme for "March Madness." Turn your bulletin board into a large basketball hoop. The background can be the backboard while using a toy basketball net to make the display more 3-D. If you are a little more ambitious, make the free-standing basketball hoop as shown on the next page using a carpet tube on a base (as described in making palm trees in Chapter 2). Use a piece of cardboard attached to the tube for the backboard and a toy net. If the net is too small, bend a coat hanger into a circle. Attach this to the cardboard and tube. Use an old fishing net that you string along the hanger for the basket.

Add a few lightweight books or magazines to the basket and books along the base. Add some appropriate slogan such as:

HOOP IT UP WITH READING!

SCORE BIG!! READ!

DON'T PASS UP A GOOD BOOK.

SLAM, DUNK, READ!!!

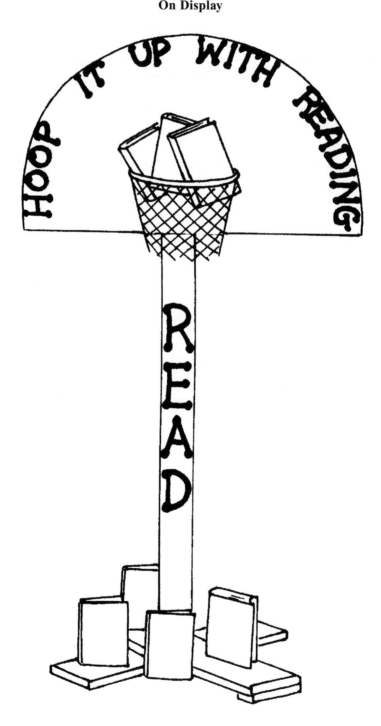

Use the names of professional basketball teams and their mascots on posterboard jerseys. Use a different one in each Dewey area with that number on the jersey. If jerseys are too much trouble to make, just make a pennant for each Dewey number area.

Use masking tape to give the floor area the look of a basketball court. Make basketballs from brown construction paper. Laminate these and then, using black marker, write on the names of special areas of the library such as the card catalog, reference, etc. Hang these all around the library.

To make the display on the next page, use a piece of white poster board for the backboard. The hoop is just a strip of black posterboard attached to the backboard. The net is white paper cut in a simple net design and then laminated. This can be attached to the hoop and the sides pinned down to create a cool basket. Fill this with magazines or construction paper books.

Display biographies of basketball players and books on the rules of the game. Feature periodicals on the sport. Display posters of players like Michael Jordan. Many of these are available for purchase featuring professional players promoting reading.

15

BASEBALL

Spring training time or World Series time are both great opportunities to showcase the great American pastime. It isn't even necessary to make a lot of things. Instead, use items like T-shirts with ball team logos printed on them, ball caps, gloves, bats, etc., for your decorating.

For the bulletin board on the next page, use whatever color background you desire. A real baseball mitt looks great with a construction paper book or a paperback in its grasp. Cut out a white circle for the ball with a few more paper books thrown in for good measure.

There are so many great phrases to use with book displays. These are just a few:

BECOME AN ALL-STAR READER.

READ A HOMERUN EVERY TIME.

BE THE DESIGNATED READER.

STEP UP WITH A BOOK!

Throughout the room, use ball gloves and caps to hold display books. Display titles on the rules of the game, biographies of great players and fiction books by authors such as Matt Christopher.

For a simple display idea for a long narrow space, trace around a baseball bat on to a piece of tan or light brown construction paper. Use a black marker and draw in the word READ in large puffy letters. Make these letters stretch out to fill up the length of the bat. The dot for this exclamation mark is a baseball. Cut a circle from white paper and draw in the stitching with a red marker.

Around the room use T-shirts from as many different ball teams as possible. If you have pennants or posters, use them also. Don't buy all these, ask friends and colleagues to borrow them for a short time. If you just can't borrow the real thing, make some from posterboard. Use one piece of posterboard for each shirt. Find the official team logos in a sports magazine or on the Internet. If you have a color printer, print these off to use on the shirts. If not, photocopy the logos and color them in with markers. Glue these logos on.

Display a large United States map in a location that patrons can readily see. Put a sticker or star in the location of each major league team. You might mark all the National League teams in blue and the American League cities in red.

Using masking tape, mark off the bases on the floor of the library or classroom. Home plate might be your checkout desk. Be creative as you move about the room creating a baseball game with reading incentives. Offer a prize such as popcorn for those students who read four books in a designated time period—one for each base and home. This could be a reading homerun.

Hang some baseball diamonds around the room with books in place of the bases. Laminate these for extra strength and shine. Hang some laminated poster board baseballs for an added effect.

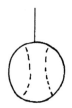

16

FOOTBALL

This is a great theme to use during Superbowl time. Feature professional and college teams with pennants and posters. Use your own school's team name with the mascot as your main focus tying it to reading. Possibly borrow a helmet and jersey from your coach to display along with biographies of great players.

Display an old school yearbook with the pages of the football team marked. Use your team colors for the total display.

Hang small plastic footballs with the word "READ" written on in black marker. The main Dewey categories could be written on these plastic footballs or some could be made from brown construction paper.

The following two pages contain simple bulletin board ideas that are basically just letters carefully arranged. Keep them very simple.

There are several good phrases to promote reading through this theme:

PUNT, PASS AND READ!

GO FOR A GOAL—READ!

TOUCHDOWN!

GET IN THE GAME ... READ!

OUR GOAL IS GOOD READING!

Use the space above a bookshelf for a football player. Keep the figure as simple as possible but consider using your school's team logo on the helmet.

Read More About FOOTBALL.

This could be a great heading for a display of football biographies or books on the rules of the game. The rectangular design would fit well over the top of a bookshelf. Use a bold color for the letters with the two footballs cut from brown construction paper trimmed with a black marker. This could give you an effective display in a very short amount of time.

17

HOPPY READING

Frogs fit in so well no matter what the time of year. Their silly expressions will bring a smile to each one who visits your library or classroom.

This "Hoppy Reading" could be done in any size. Use blue paper or blue plastic for the background with a large red construction paper book to set off the frog.

To make this cool frog for your display, use a large sheet of green construction paper or poster board. Make a pattern first by folding in half a sheet of newspaper that is the same size as your green paper. Draw half of the frog on the fold as shown in the drawing. Cut this out while the paper is still folded and use for your pattern. Cut two hands to position around a real book or paper one. Cut two large white circles for the eyes with two smaller black circles for the pupils. Use a black marker to draw on a smile. Finish off the display with large, bold letters proclaiming your message.

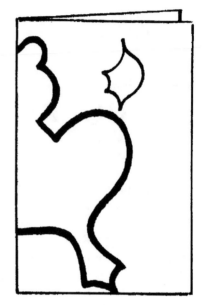

Use carpet tubes to create free-standing frogs. Cut the tube to be approximately 12" tall. To cover the end of the tube, use a square of green paper. Fold down the paper over the sides of the tube and tape it down tightly. Cover the tube with a rectangle of green paper that covers the taped area. Glue down the ends.

To make the frog legs as shown on the next page, use a piece of newspaper to make a pattern. Be sure to add a small space along the inside of the leg to have something to attach to the tube. Trace around your pattern onto a large sheet of green paper or poster board. Use markers or crayons to add some lines and color to the legs.

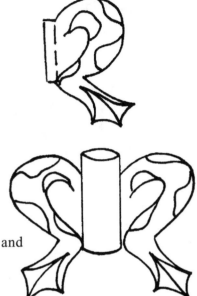

Position the legs on the tube and glue in place.

Keep the head as simple as possible. Start with a green circle. Add two white ovals for eyeballs with smaller black circles for pupils. Use a marker to add a smile. Use a yellow or green marker to add some dots of color to the face. Do the same to the tube between the leg sections.

Glue the head on the front of the tube so that it sticks up above the tube.

To make the front legs, fold a sheet of 9" × 12" green paper in half. Draw a leg shape and cut it out while the paper is still folded. Use a marker to add some spots of color.

A book can be placed in the frog's hands or the frog can just stand alone. Give it a lily pad to complete the picture. A lily pad is just a circle with a pie-shaped piece cut out.

If you do not have access to carpet tubes or want a lighter weight frog, try this. Begin with a rectangle of green paper.

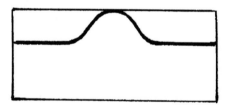

Glue the ends of the piece together.

Add large white ovals for eyes with smaller black circles for the pupils. Draw on a smile.

Use two long strips of green paper for the legs. Cut both pieces of paper at the same time so that both legs will match. Use markers or crayons to add some spots and color to the legs.

Glue the top of the leg to the body tube. Bend the leg around and tack with a small dot of glue. Repeat this on the other side with the other leg. Make front legs as previously described.

These can also become jumping frogs. The difference will be in the way you glue on the legs.

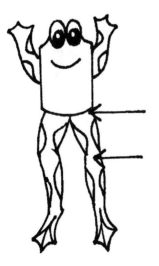

Glue the legs inside the tube and allow them to hang down. Bend the paper at the knee and ankle area.

"GET A JUMP ON YOUR READING"

For this "Hoppy New Year" idea, use the frogs as they are or add bowties and top hats for a little more pizzazz. Create 3-D frogs following the directions previously given. Use blue paper for the background and blue plastic for the water.

Make frog heads from green paper plates or a circle of green construction paper. Add eyes and a big smile. Suspend it from the ceiling with fishing line.

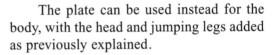

The plate can be used instead for the body, with the head and jumping legs added as previously explained.

Try a display heading such as:

READING MAKES ME "HOPPY"!

BOOKS WE'D CROAK FOR!

These are some great children's books to feature:

Seven Froggies Went to School.
Picasso, the Green Tree Frog.
Frog Counts to Ten.
Frog and Toad are Friends.
Flashy Fantastic Rain Forest Frogs.
Tuesday.

18

FAIRY TALES

Fairy tales are so appealing to any age group. These can be the basis for a great theme or unit of study. The story of Cinderella has been done in over 1500 versions. Feature books such as

The Egyptian Cinderella.
Cinderlad.
Sidney Rella and the Glass Sneaker.
Princess Furball.
Yeh Shen.
The Korean Cinderella.

How about *The Three Bears* or *The Three Little Pigs? The True Story of the Three Little Pigs* by A. Wolf is really fun to read and to teach point-of-view. *Lon Po Po* is the Chinese version of *Little Red Riding Hood*. These are all so entertaining.

Turning your room into a castle will capture the imaginations of your patrons. Use long sheets of white paper to simulate the stone castle walls. The top of the wall all around the room is really the most important. Use a black marker or black paint to draw in the blocks. Don't make them precise and square—round off the corners and be creative. Cut across the center to create two sections of usable rocks at the same time. Splatter them lightly with black, brown and tan paint.

Towers can be created by making the
rocks work vertically. Create it in the same
way as previously described starting with a
rectangle of paper. Curve the rocks slightly.

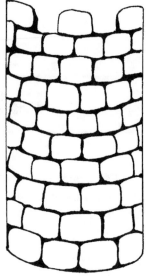

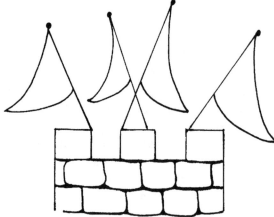

To decorate your
new castle, add flags
and pennants. Use
dowel rods or balloon
sticks for these.

Large banners can be made from
brightly colored poster paper and hung
from the ceiling. Research the Middle
Ages for heraldry ideas.

Over the doorways, create simple arches. Make an arch out of paper to fit over the top of the door. Use a marker to outline the rocks. White lights can be used to outline the castle walls or the arched doorway.

Feature books on knights, knighthood, King Arthur, Merlin, chivalry, armor and dragons.

St. George and the Dragon.
The Flying Dragon Room.
King Arthur and the Knights of the Round Table.
Excalibur.
The Dragons Are Singing Tonight.

Once Upon A Time...

The bulletin board on the next page is great for this theme. The castle is simple to make and will look great!

Blues and purples are good fantasy colors. Either would make a terrific background. Gray paper is best for the castle. The castle is just two rectangles and a square. Add two triangles for the top of the towers. Cut out the small squares along the top of the big square. Add a door from dark paper or just color in the space with a marker. Add some rocks around the door opening. Add a few small pennants.

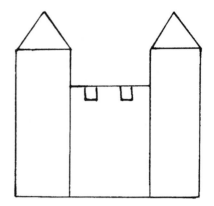

Use polyfil or cotton to create a cloud for the castle to be floating on. Make the letters from black or a silver metallic paper.

This decorating theme can be the basis for gothic romance novels for your more sophisticated patrons. You might title this:

GOOD KNIGHT READING!

To further promote the fairy tale/tall tale section of your library, consider a simple design like the one on the following page. Use a black marker and a yardstick to draw in the word TALL. Make the letters very tall and use shorter, fatter letters for the word TALES. Add an additional message as to their location in your library.

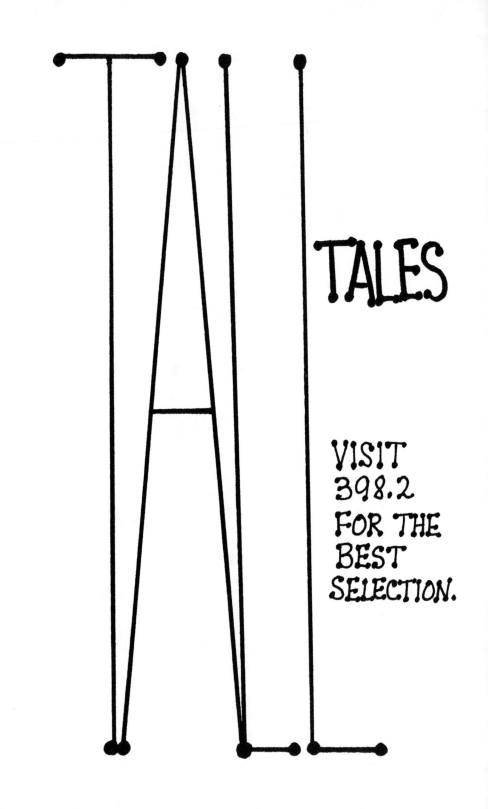

TALL TALES

VISIT
398.2
FOR THE
BEST
SELECTION.

19

THE WEATHER

Everyone talks about the weather and everyone always has an opinion about it. Use this as your decorating theme featuring every kind of weather at once.

For the display idea below, the background would probably be best done in blue with bright colors for the books and accessories.

Feature a different type of weather in each corner of the room with another in the center. In one area, create a tornado. This can be done by simply hanging a large sheet of paper with the tornado drawn on in marker with a few books or magazines added. Hang some additional paper books or newspapers on fishing line in the area to simulate the tornado. Tape strips of tissue paper to a fan in this area for the appearance and sound of the wind.

Let it snow in another corner. Cut snowflakes of different sizes from white paper and laminate them if possible. Hang these with fishing line throughout the area. Create some reading snow people from poster paper that appear to be sitting along the top of your book shelves or make them lifesize for a large open wall space.

Rain can be the focus of another area. Make blue construction paper raindrops that you laminate. Not only does the lamination make them stronger, but the shine creates a more water-like look. Hang several real umbrellas from the ceiling and use a few to create a book display.

BOOKS FOR A RAINY DAY

Feature lots of sunshine in the last corner. Make a large reading sun complete with sunglasses from yellow poster paper. Hang lots of small suns throughout the area.

Make sure that this area is well lit. Extra lighting might be needed to give the appearance of sunshine.

This would be a great area to set up a display of books that have a weather term in the title. These are elementary titles but many more mature titles could be substituted.

Cloudy with a Chance of Meatballs.
On Sunday the Wind Came.
The Magic School Bus Inside a Hurricane.
The Rainbow Fish.
The Rain Mouse.
The Sun Is a Golden Earring.
The Snowy Day.

Today's Forecast: A Great Day For Reading!

In the center of the room, hang some clouds with some lightning bolts thrown in. The clouds can be made from white poster board or use white ½" or ¾" foam insulation sheets. These are available at lumber yards in 4' × 8' pieces and can easily be cut with a matte knife or utility knife. This material is very lightweight and will hang easily with fishing line. Lightning can also be made of this and painted or just use yellow poster board.

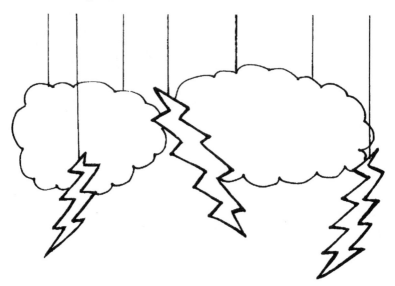

Use a piece of foamboard to cut an arch to create a rainbow. Paint this and attach a cloud at each end. The rainbow can also be made from paper and put flat on the wall.

20

GEOGRAPHY

Our students need to improve their geography skills. To call attention to our world and many of its parts, feature everything you have on maps, travel, atlases and globes. Check with your state's tourism department or highway department for maps of your state to hand out to your patrons.

The bulletin board ideas on the next two pages are very simple to create with limited resources. The first is just a world map set on any color background paper with some black letters added.

For the other idea, cut the letters for the word READ from some out-of-date maps. Position them on a black background making the letters as large as possible.

Visit a travel company to borrow some posters of a variety of travel destinations. Use these throughout the room along with books about that spot. Plan ahead of time and send a postcard to each state's travel bureau to request travel information (email if that is possible). These will add a lot later to your vertical file and will be great for your decorating.

Create a treasure hunt by using clues about places around the world. These could lead to books on various destinations and prizes might be given to those who complete the hunt.

For a different twist to this theme, use a large United States map. Feature different states throughout the room changing them every few days. This could be done to create a trivia game asking questions about the states moving from one coast to the other.

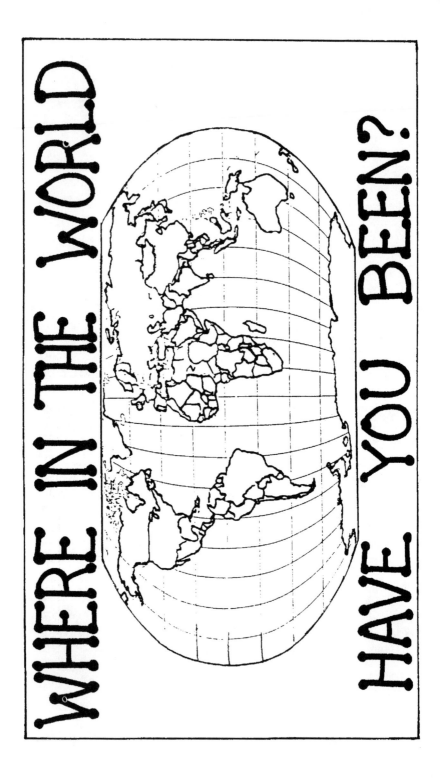

WHERE IN THE WORLD HAVE YOU BEEN?

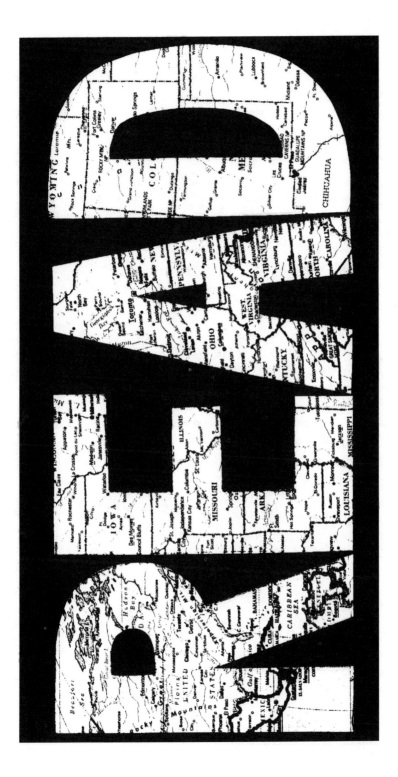

The inside cover of *World Almanac for Kids* features the license plates of all 50 states. Choose some to photocopy and enlarge. Add a little color with markers and laminate them. Use a permanent marker to add Dewey number headings or label them with titles such as biographies, mysteries, etc. These will add to your travel theme and help to call attention to specific books.

Old highway maps can be used to cover boxes, like wrapping paper. These can be used to display books or work as bookends.

Put a masking tape equator on the floor down the center of your room. Put up a sign on the west side of the room that says Western Hemisphere and put Eastern Hemisphere on the opposite side. Mark north, south, east and west. Create a globe with your library as the center of the world. Mark the International Dateline, etc., possibly even noting time zones and the time differences as they relate to your location.

Use a globe as the center of a book display featuring books from all parts of the world. Use some post-it notes or small stickers to mark on the globe the locations featured in the displayed books. Use a large world map as a cover for the table upon which to build your display. This will be a great looking display with very little effort on your part.

Feature some cool travel web sites for your net surfers. Find some reputable email penpals to hook up a classroom in your school to a classroom in another country.

Another simple display tool is the suitcase. Use several around the room to call attention to various travel areas such as the Caribbean or the mountains. As in the illustration on the following page, use open suitcases and fill them with books featuring different travel locations.

To add to this idea, create a simple construction paper book complete with arms, legs, suitcase and shades. This little character will fit in well no matter what the size.

This would be a great way to display books, magazines or vertical file travel information on warm getaway locations. Add some props such as a large sunhat, a suitcase, sunglasses, a beach towel, maybe some sand, seashells, lotion, etc. Keep the display simple using things you already have on hand. The only thing you would really have to make would be a large bright sun and some letters for your message.

The same idea could be used to focus on cold climates. Use a suitcase once again and fill it with books on skiing, mountain climbing, Mt. Everest, the Arctic, etc.

Add props such as a warm scarf, earmuffs, stocking caps, and white paper to serve as snow. Cut snowflakes and laminate them for the extra shine. Hang these throughout the display.

COOL CLIMATE
WARM READING!

21

GREAT IDEAS

Our world is built upon hundreds of great ideas. Every modern convenience we use, every form of transportation, even much of the food we eat began as someone's great idea. Feature these throughout your library to inspire some creative thinking in your patrons.

For the bulletin board on the next page, use poster paper in bright colors to create a boy or girl or use your school mascot. The head is just a large circle. Facial features can be added with cut paper or simply drawn in with markers. Add some cut paper hair. Trace around your hands to create the hands to hold a paper book or a magazine.

Use white paper for the cloud-like shape above the head with a bright yellow lightbulb. Black letters will make the words very obvious.

Hang laminated lightbulbs around the room with fishing line to emphasize the "light" coming on. Use yellow paper for the top of the bulb with the filament drawn in with black marker. Use aluminum foil for the bottom of the bulb.

Choose a few simple inventions to showcase such as the ice cream cone or the game of basketball. These might be some good display headings:

EUREKA!

WHY DIDN'T I THINK OF THAT?

WHAT A GREAT IDEA!

WISH I WOULD HAVE THOUGHT OF THAT!

COOL IDEA!

Choose a great idea to feature in each Dewey area. This can be done by using a poster or simple sign to list the idea and a possible date.

000 — The invention of the computer.
100 — Philosophy. This is a personal belief call but maybe you might feature something by Dr. Spock.
200 — All of the religions most common to your patrons.
300 — Democracy.
400 — Our alphabet.
500 — Mathematics or any cool physics theory.
600 — This whole section is full of tons of great inventions. Lasers, rockets, NASA, automobiles, trains, etc.
700 — Paintings by Vincent Van Gogh or baseball.
800 — The works of William Shakespeare.
900 — The end of slavery in the United States or possibly the Louisiana Purchase.

Feature biographies of famous inventors or great thinkers such as:

Thomas Edison
Albert Einstein
Socrates
Isaac Newton
Henry Ford
Leonardo da Vinci

Create a time line to go around your room starting from the earliest recorded time through the present, picking out a few key inventions or ideas. Use a computer to generate the words and photographs or just write them in with a marker and cut pictures from magazines.

Consider sponsoring a contest for the product that the world has been waiting for. Require a drawing of the proposed product and a written description explaining why we need it. Award a book or a small bookstore gift certificate to the most creative inventor.

A great game for this theme is pictionary. Use the names of great inventions such as laser, microwave, motorcycle, pizza, etc. This game is played with two teams taking turns drawing pictures that will make it possible for their team to guess the correct word. The team gets a point for each correct guess. The team with the most points is the winner.

22

COMICS, PUZZLES
AND JOKES

April is national humor month. Laughter is often in short supply these days so promote it the whole month long with a joke-a-day, a trivia contest similar to the Jeopardy television program and some word puzzles.

You will probably be surprised at how many joke and riddle books you have in your library. The 800s are home to many great humor books to feature with this theme including poetry books by Shel Silverstein or Ogden Nash.

Write out some short riddles or knock-knock jokes and display them around the room. Create some bockmarks on your computer that you can photocopy and distribute during the month which feature book jokes or reading related riddles. Make several large smiling mouths to laminate and hang around the room. Write in your favorite joke or riddle.

GO AHEAD...
LAUGH IF
YOU WANT TO.

APRIL IS NATIONAL
HUMOR MONTH!

National Library Week is celebrated during April and is an excellent opportunity to host a Jeopardy game. The purpose of this is not to push winning but to encourage your students to use the library's resources to find information. This game can be played in two ways. For older students, create five questions for each day. Try to use a wide range of topics and all must be possible to answer using the reference materials in your library. All answers must be in the form of a question as on the television program.

Devise an official answer sheet that has a space for the time the paper is turned in. The winner is the student who has the most correct responses in the shortest amount of time. Give one prize each day. Many fast food restaurants will donate food coupons to use as prizes. This will save you money and is good advertising for them.

Your faculty and staff will want to participate also so create a really difficult question each day for them. One is probably all they will have time to attempt.

The World Almanac is a great source of possible questions. These are some examples:

The nickname for the state of Nebraska. (What is the cornhusker state?)

The name or term used for a young pigeon. (What is a squab?)

The tallest mountain in the United States. (What is Mt. McKinley?)

For younger children, use only one or two questions each day with a small prize for each one who enters. This could be a piece of candy or a small bookmark.

It is easy to create word searches or crossword puzzles for your patrons. There are some crossword puzzle computer programs you can use or make a simple one yourself. Feature words that have been a part of your library skills lessons.

You can create a bulletin board crossword puzzle such as the one on the next page quite easily. Computer generate the clues and leave the boxes of the puzzle blank to get your patrons to think.

ACROSS

1. A teacher of library skills.
3. The story of a person's life.
5. Up-to-date information on many topics squeezed into one volume. It is published each year.
7. Material that is not true.

DOWN

1. The place to check out books, magazines, newspapers, videos, etc.
2. Information that can be fiction or nonfiction.
4. A book of maps.
6. Computer access to information all over the world.

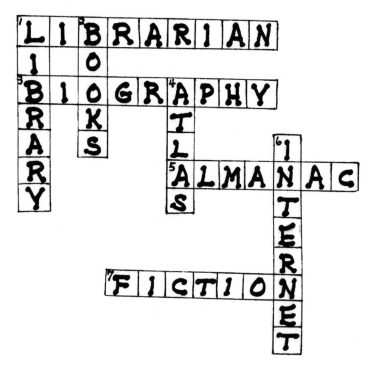

Word search puzzles are always popular. Photocopy them to pass out to patrons.

Library Word Search

```
E A S C O M P U T E R O G L I N K
P I R H L U A N R S S T I L E M O
A L T A V I S T A D R A H U T I B
C A W T I N P G U K M O J P I V E
S C W E L T O D N E B K Y N S C W
T R O Y P E D S T X I R H D A B E
E V R A N R T K I C H O O O H A Y
N A L G O N E O L I S W M I W X I
I B D W H E K Y M T A I E H Q U L
W F Y U S T C A W E P E P J E R C
X E R O J O F G K L U N A N K T E
K T F S S E A R C H E N G I N E S
Z N U D A T M U X N V W E Z U H C
I L C H B L G P A S U B J E C T R
Y N T I N F O R M A T I O N E T O
O N L I N E D H Y P R O T Y S O L
T A W E B C R A W L E R S L U J L
```

Can you find these words in the puzzle above:

NETSCAPE	NETWORK
ALTAVISTA	ONLINE
INFOSEEK	KEYWORD
EXCITE	SUBJECT
EMAIL	
LINK	
INTERNET	
WEBCRAWLER	
CHAT	
YAHOO	
LYCOS	
SEARCH ENGINES	
WEB	
SCROLL	
WORLD	
HOME PAGE	
SITE	
INFORMATION	
COMPUTER	

    In the 700s we find great comic strip books featuring Garfield, Snoopy, Spiderman, Superman, etc. Display these along with comic strips from the Sunday newspaper.

    A whole theme could be built around the super heroes of the comic books. How about using Spiderman or Batman to promote reading. Use the "POW" or "ZAP" concept with words like:

Smile—it will be contagious!

23

THE INTERNET

The Internet is like a giant magnet to most students. They are just drawn to it to search out endless possibilities. It is a little difficult to decorate for, however. For a totally simple sign, try this one done on poster paper in marker.

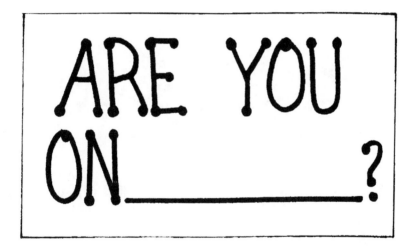

Use Halloween spider webs that can be stretched and pulled apart to create a wall-sized web or simply draw one in marker on a large sheet of paper. A spider will serve as your web walker. Use a large rubber spider or make one from construction paper. A 3-D spider can be made from two sizes of styrofoam balls attached together and painted black with furry, fat pipe cleaners for the legs. Hang this on fishing line.

List all kinds of appealing web sites on poster board that you have laminated for durability. Attach these to the web. Hang some additional spiders on fishing line from the ceiling in front of the web.

This same concept works with the cool "net" sites explained in Chapter 5 and search engines featured in Chapter 3. Using the Internet requires learning about search engines. Feature the most often used ones on the wall above or near your computers. Either of these will help to promote the Internet.

Surfing the net is fun but often a little scary for first time users. Encourage your patrons to be surfers. Make large waves out of blue paper to cover the wall space behind the Internet computers. Make a version of the bulletin board on the next page using blue paper for the waves and a surf board with a simple, stereotyped version of a computer. This just needs to be an impression of a computer so it does not need to be fancy.

A palm tree (as explained in Chapter 2) positioned next to the computers would add to the atmosphere. Cover the chairs at the computer stations with beach towels.

The Internet is called the information super highway. Create a simple road and sign scene to promote this. Use blue poster paper for the background and gray for the road. Add signs promoting some search engines. See the drawing for this display on the following page.

Encourage your patrons to read about the Internet and learn more about all its possibilities. The bulletin board featuring a computer sitting on a stack of books (page 146) might just be the right visual to bring this about. Display books, magazines and videos about the Internet. Offer helpful search hints on handout sheets.

24

BEE A READER

Every day we are surrounded by all types of insects. Feature a few of the most commonly accepted ones such as bumblebees and ladybugs. Both of these are bright colors that will work well for decorating purposes. Make them much larger than life and as friendly looking as possible.

For the bulletin board on the next page, use lots of bright flowers and colorful books to showcase your reading bumblebee. Directions for making the bee will be given in this chapter.

Work on a large scale using lots of flowers for this display to serve as resting places for your bees and ladybugs. Simple flowers like daisies can be made from poster board and hung from the ceiling with fishing line. Glue a center on each side so they will look good all the way around as they turn and spin in the breeze.

Great 3-D bumblebees can be made from black and yellow construction paper. Cut the basic body shape from yellow paper and add the black stripes with black paper or in black marker.

Add six legs. These can be just thin strips of black construction paper attached in the center section of the bug. Add two antennae and two black circles for eyes. Bend the legs down under the bee and make it stand up.

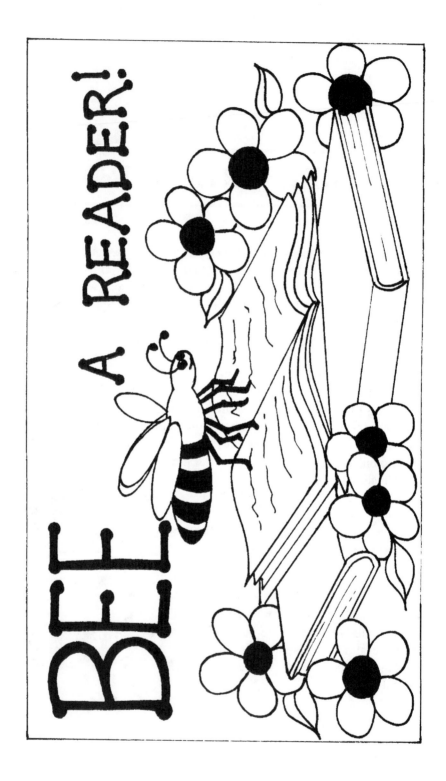

The four wings are made from wax paper. Position these bees on flowers and books throughout the room.

A 3-D bee can be made from a tube of yellow construction paper. Roll a small piece of yellow paper into a cone.

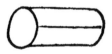

Slide it through the tube and tape it in the inside to form the stinger. Add some stripes of black paper or draw them in with a black marker.

The head is an oval shape with a slight point on the bottom. Add two large circles for eyes and two antennae. Add a little tab to each side of the head to be able to attach it to the inside of the tube body. Glue the head on.

Add six legs made from construction paper or furry black pipe cleaners.

Cut four wings from wax paper. To make really cool wings, use florist wire that has been covered in florist tape and fold it into a V shape. Put this between laminating film and laminate. Cut the wing shape out. The wire will allow you to bend it and shape the wing into the desired position.

Punch the wire through the paper carefully and twist the end so it will hold the wing in place. If using wax paper wings, glue these on with the two front wings slightly overlapping the back ones. Wax paper looks so cool for these and is an inexpensive material.

Hang your bees on fishing line around the room. These will look fabulous leading the way to a book display. One of these headings might fit your needs.

MAKE A BEE-LINE TO THE NEW BOOKS!

A "HONEY" OF A GOOD BOOK.

BUZZ OFF—I'M READING!

MAKE A BEE-LINE TO THE NEW BOOKS.

Ladybugs are always so popular and they appear to be friendly. Use red and black construction paper for these bugs. Start with a black base shape. Glue on red paper to cover 3/4 of this shape. Just glue on the piece, turn it over and trim away the extra.

Add six legs, two eyes and a couple of cool antennae. Position these all over the room.

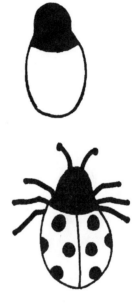

BUGGED BY WHAT TO READ?
TRY ONE OF THESE:

Create a display of fiction and nonfiction books about insects. *The Bee Tree, The Very Grouchy Ladybug,* and *Sarah's Story* are great along with books on beetles, ants, and butterflies. Emphasize the uniqueness and beauty of these insects rather than the pest aspect.

25

HATS OFF TO READING

This theme is great if you don't feel confident making decorator items. Spend some time collecting hats of all types and sizes, borrowing some if possible from all different kinds of professions. Consider also using some from Halloween costumes such as a witch's hat, princess's pointed hat, or a clown hat.

a football helmet

a nurse's hat

a fireman's helmet

a police hat

a hard hat

a baseball cap

a hat from a military uniform

a cowboy hat

a large sunbonnet

a space helmet

a magician's hat or top hat

a chef's hat

a baby bonnet

a beanie

a "Cat in the Hat" type hat

a bowler

a pith helmet

a turban

a coonskin cap

a Santa hat

To make the bulletin board on the next page, use real hats pinned into place among paper books. This will give a 3-D look to the display. Hats can also be hung with fishing line to give the appearance that they have blown away from their owners.

HOLD ON TO YOUR HAT!

WE HAVE SOME GREAT NEW BOOKS!

Check with your school's counselor and see if a career day is planned. If not, plan one and feature hats and books on a wide variety of career options. Use the hats themselves to hold books or let the books wear the hats.

Make top hats from gallon cans. The cafeteria would probably save some of these for you if you ask. Cover the can in black paper. Set the can on a larger sheet of black paper. Trace around the bottom. Using a compass or ruler, measure 6" out from your traced circle to create a hat brim. Cut this out and slide it over the can. A ribbon or stripe of a contrasting color will make a great hatband.

With the top open, use this as a flower pot or vase. Smaller versions of this can become pencil cans or hold scrap paper.

Invert the can and cover the bottom in black paper, pulling it down tightly and taping it in place.

Cover the sides with a rectangle of black paper. Make the brim as previously described and slide it on over the top. Use this as a book display stand.

These might be some activities to consider as you plan this display:

1. Sponsor a hat day offering a prize for the most unusual hat. This would be great fun as a way to beat those wintertime blahs. We all need to laugh more and enjoy a simple activity such as this.

2. *The Cat in the Hat* could be your featured book with lots of possibilities such as a Dr. Seuss reading marathon or a pet show.

3. Feature your magic books, displaying them with one of your "can" top hats.

INDEX

161

Index